SCrAP It!

Using scrapbooking techniques for
decorative and gift items.

Jaclyn Venter

SCrAP It!

Using scrapbooking techniques for decorative and gift items.

Jaclyn Venter

STACKPOLE BOOKS

*Dedicated to my darling
husband, Carlo. You've been
with me every step of the
way supporting me as ideas
turned into projects. You are
my greatest inspiration and
motivation and I am forever
grateful that you allow me
to be the best that I can be.
My life is full because you
are part of it. I love you.*

Published by Stackpole Books
5067 Ritter Road
Mechanicsburg, PA 17055
www.stackpolebooks.com

First published in 2011
by Metz Press
1 Cameronians Avenue
Welgemoed, 7530 South Africa

Publisher and editor: Wilsia Metz
Photography: Ivan Naudé
Design and layout: Liezl Maree
Proofreader: Deborah Morbin
Print production: Robert Wong,
    Color/Fuzion
Pinted and bound by
    Tien Wah Press, Singapore

ISBN: 978-0-8117-1268-2

Contents

Where do I scrapbook?
My dear husband spoiled me in 2010 with a fully kitted craft studio in our home. I spend most of my time in here or in the kitchen cooking and baking, yet another passion of mine.

Favourite part of the studio?
I have a beautiful red cupboard with 35 little drawers where I keep all my scrapbooking supplies like brads, flowers and chalk.

Favourite tool?
My Fiskars upper crest border punch and my pink Fiskars craft mat.

Favourite project to scrap?
Mini books! All kinds of mini books, Starbucks coffee cup mini books, canvas, felt – mini books.

Favourite paper brand?
Heidi Grace
Dear Lizzy by Advantus
Heidi Swapp

Must haves in my life?
PINK everything, kettle, scrapbooking tools, jewellery and Starbucks coffee.

Introduction

The book

Introductions are as much about authors as they are about books, so let me first introduce myself.

I live in Centurion, Pretoria, with my husband of eight years, where taking photos, paper and glue all fill my life and give it meaning. I have a passion for crafting and my creativity is fed by my family and friends who allow me to live my dream.

I am a Fiskars-certified brand ambassador, better known as Fisk-a-teer #1287. A Fiskateer is an ambassador for crafting and for Fiskars, and I am part of this global programme, teaching all of the Fiskars scrapbooking classes in South Africa.

You may have seen my face or my name on various local and international online media, the *Show me how* craft programme on the Home channel of DSTV and various blogs.

This book is about traditional scrapbooking with a twist – a do-it-yourself book where you apply ordinary scrapbooking techniques to everyday items, turning them into gorgeous gifts or decorative items for your home. Rather than making the usual scrapbook pages, sitting in an album that many people may never see or take an interest in, you use the techniques for off-the-page scrapbooking, or simply altered items.

The idea of the book originated from my love for paper and glue combined with tins, mini books, coffee cups and frames – all items that can be scrapbooked – and grew to include just about everything but the kitchen sink. Once you start looking around you, the sky is the limit as to what can be altered using scrapbooking techniques. And the sky is only the limit because I cannot reach it!

In this book I will teach you to transform everyday household items into beautiful crafty objects, adding a twist to the ordinary. The focus remains on preserving memories, and you will use lots of photographs, patterned paper, journalling, stamps, shapes, ribbon and every imaginable scrapbook tool and element. The difference is that you will create items to be put on display for all to see – either for yourself or as much appreciated gifts for friends and loved ones.

I hope I will inspire you to start crafting memorable altered items by following my step-by-step instructions – to share everyday stories with everyday items, from a scrapbooked handbag to a memory hanger. There is so much more to scrapbooking than piles and piles of albums. Grab your tools and join me on a journey of fun creating memories you can truly share.

Supplies

Here is a list of the basic items I used to make the projects in this book. These supplies can be found at any craft or scrapbook store. If you find any items that suit you better, by all means use them and have fun.

Adhesive

I absolutely adore refillable tape runners because it is quick and easy to use them. I prefer 3L E-Z Runner to ensure that my paper, chipboard or embellishments are glued down securely.

Dodz are small, double-sided adhesive circles that are available in a variety of sizes and in 3D.

Liquid glue is used to adhere anything from metal to paper. It normally has two applicators and is acid-free.

Paint

Craft paint, PVA and spray paint can be applied to any item including wood and metal. Just remember to give the item a good sanding before applying the paint. Some items may need a primer or base coat.

Paintbrushes and applicators

I used brushes and sponge applicators to paint projects. A sponge applicator generally gives a smoother finish. Clean both applicators and brushes thoroughly after use so they will last longer.

Brads

These metal fasteners are great to hold flowers, paper or photos in place, at the same time adding a decorative touch.

Cardstock

Thick, acid free paper available in many colours, plain and patterned.

Chipboard

Thick or thin cardboard used to give structure or durability to projects.

Patterned paper

Coordinating paper combinations that are available in a variety of designs and styles.

Ribbon

You can tie things together with ribbon or use it simply for decoration but it is a beautiful and useful element to add spark to any project. Visit haberdasheries and fabric shops to scout for off-cuts of ribbon and lace at bargain prices.

Rub-ons

These can be titles, words, borders or patterns and are transferred to any object like wood, paper, tin or glass.

Miscellaneous

Use anything you wish as your base or to decorate items you wish to alter – and don't be scared to experiment. That's how the greatest ideas are born.

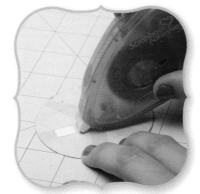

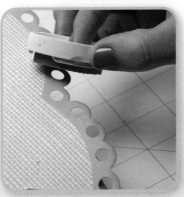

Tools

The tools listed are mainly from Fiskars but you could use whatever you have instead. These tools just make the crafting experience easier. I certainly cannot get by without my paper trimmer and the Ultra ShapeXpress™!

Craft knife

I use the Fiskars finger craft knife – an inexpensive, indispensible tool that trims paper and assists in cutting chipboard.

Craft mat

Mine is a 30 x 45 cm (12 x 18 in) self-healing mat with measuring on both sides. I prefer Fiskars and they also have it in pink.

Bone folder

It is a plastic tool that helps you score paper and can also be used to apply rub-ons.

Craft hand-drill

I use a Fiskars craft hand-drill to drill through wood and plastic. It is hand-powered and has a variety of drill bits to suit your crafting needs.

Hand punches

Fiskars offers a large variety of hand punches. Use what you have.

Computer

I use mine to create titles and text for various projects in Microsoft word. Use whichever program you are familiar with, and experiment with the many available fonts.

Lever punches

Fiskars lever punches come in a variety of sizes and are easy to use.

Paper piercer

I used Heidi Swapp's petite piercer because it is small and fits easily into my craft bag. It is a sharp tool with a needle point that pokes holes into paper, material and felt.

Sanding block

A foam core block that provides a rough surface.

Squeeze punch

These hand punches are unique in that you squeeze the handles together to punch. I used the Fiskars large circle punch.

Trimmer

I endorse the Fiskars Euro 12" trimmer because of its durability and cutting perfection. The accuracy of your trimming often determines the success of your project. If you do not have a trimmer, a ruler (preferably metal), scissors or craft knife and pencil will help you do the job too, albeit with considerably more effort.

Ultra ShapeXpress™

Cut fun shapes, alphabets and borders or work free-hand with this unique 360° blade tool. It works well with Fiskars templates. I used the heart and circle templates for projects throughout the book. If you do not have the Ultra ShapeXpress, find templates of various shapes, as these always come in handy.

Projects

Serving trays

YOU WILL NEED

Trimmer
Craft mat
Ultra ShapeXpress™
Circle and super-sized circle template set
4 wood serving trays
Sandpaper
Paint
Paintbrush
4 sheets of patterned paper (I used Bo Bunny)
4 sheets of Couture cardstock
Chalk ink (I used VersaMagic)
Scrapbook adhesives (I used 3L E-Z Runner)
Chipboard letters (I used Heidi Grace)

I searched for the perfect serving tray and found these at a very affordable price at a second-hand store. I love the idea of setting a beautiful breakfast or lunch table for friends and family. The trays are personalised with paper and embellishments and you could add a name or photos as well. They will most definitely be the talk of the table and make a lovely gift.

1 Sand the wooden trays with sandpaper to remove any dirt or old paint to prepare the surface for painting. Wipe away any dust and particles.

2 Apply several layers of paint to the serving trays, allowing them to dry between layers. Put the trays aside to dry properly.

3 Select patterned paper for each tray and cut circles according to the size of the shapes on your trays. I used the Fiskars Ultra ShapeXpress™ and Fiskars Shape Template set of super-sized circles to cut a 21 cm (8.25 in) and a 7,6 cm (3 in) circle.

4 Using the VersaMagic chalk ink, chalk the edges of the circles.

5 Using the scrapbook adhesives, adhere the paper circles in the circles of the serving tray.

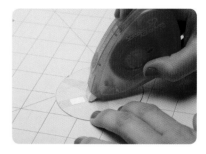

6 Form the word *yum* in chipboard letters and stick down on the serving tray.

7 Type inspirational food quotes in Microsoft Word and print it on cardstock. Cut the cardstock to fit the cutlery space on the serving tray and stick down.

Home printer's tray

1 Paint the printer's tray brown and allow to dry. Apply more than one coat of paint if necessary, allowing enough drying time between coats.

2 Use the cream craft paint to dry-brush the sides and inner panels.

3 Attach the door handle to the top of the printer's tray.

4 Measure each block of the printer's tray and cut patterned paper to size. Chalk the edges and stick down.

5 Finally use photos and embellishments to decorate your printer's tray and display it in your hallway or a special place in your home.

A printer's tray is an easily accessible wooden product. You will find blanks at any good craft store or paint shop. The story I tell with this printer's tray is about what makes a house a home. You can portray any theme in a similar way by adapting your colours, paper selection and embellishments.

A tin of notes

YOU WILL NEED

Trimmer

Craft mat

A 14 x 17 cm tin

3 sheets of patterned paper
(I used My mind's eye)

Ruler

Length of ribbon, 2,5 cm
(1 in) wide

Chipboard letters

Mini notebook that fits the tin

Chalk

Scrapbook adhesive

Pen

Tins make very versatile gifts – they can be used and decorated in several ways and this idea is only one of many. Although these tins are widely available as blanks you can also recycle old tins and give them a new lease on life by applying beautiful papers and embellishments using scrapbooking techniques. Everybody makes notes and to do lists, and losing these could be quite frustrating. I decided to store my notes and pen in a scrapbooked tin.

1 Measure the lid and bottom of your tin and cut patterned paper to fit the sizes measured. Round the corners of the paper, chalk the edges and adhere to the lid (top and inside) and the bottom (inside) of the tin.

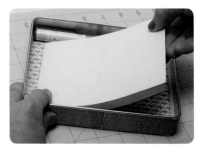

2 Measure the sides of the tin and the lid and cut patterned paper to go round. Chalk the edges and adhere to the sides of the tin and the lid.

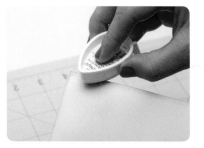

3 Chalk the edges of you mini note book and adhere in the middle of the bottom part of the tin. Add a pen.

4 Cut two triangles from contrasting patterned paper and stick them into the lid of the tin to form a pocket. Only place adhesive on one side and the bottom of each triangle so that you can slip notes, bills, invoices or photos into the pocket.

5 Finally chalk the chipboard letters and adhere them to the top of the tin. Place a ribbon around the tin and tie a beautiful bow.

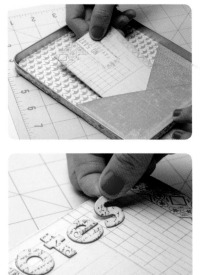

Lamps with a twist

YOU WILL NEED

Trimmer
Craft mat
2 lamps
Patterned paper
Cardstock
Ruler
Rub-ons
Ribbon or rick-rack
Buttons
Clear heart
Scrapbook adhesive
Chalk

1 Measure the inside windows of the lamp and cut patterned paper to size, chalk the edges and place inside your lamp.

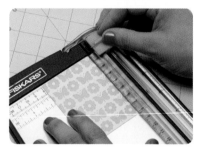

2 Print your photos to size, mat, finish with ribbon and rub-ons and adhere to the patterned paper in one or two windows.

3 Print the title *You light up my life* on cardstock, cut out and adhere to the lamps. I used hearts, matted some words, and added rub-ons.

4 Embellish the outside of the lamp with more shapes, ribbon and buttons.

Mini lamps bring beautiful light to our homes. But why not give them a twist and add a photo of the person who lights up your life, as well as other embellishments to turn them into unique decor pieces. These and similar lamps are readily available from several home stores.

Fridge magnets

So who said you couldn't scrap your fridge? Scrapped fridge magnets are a great way of decorating your fridge and so easy to do. Making the fridge magnets out of a take-away coffee-cup sleeve is even more special, and you will be doing your bit for the environment by recycling. The circles are not big, so you can also use up any scraps of patterned paper. I enjoyed this project a lot because of my love for coffee.

1 Punch six scalloped circles using the patterned paper.

2 Punch six scalloped circles of the same size using the coffee-cup sleeves.

3 Glue the paper circles to the smooth side of the coffee-cup sleeves.

4 Cut the ribbon into suitable lengths, fold and glue to the back of the circles, then chalk the edges of the circles.

5 Punch suitable words using the labelmaker, and stick them onto the front of the circles.

6 Cut six pieces of magnetic strip and adhere to the back of the circles, covering the folded ribbon. Allow to dry thoroughly and display on your fridge.

Magazine holders

YOU WILL NEED

Trimmer

Craft mat

Magazine-holder blanks
11 x 26,5cm (4.3 x 10.4 in)

Paint in your colour of choice

Patterned paper
(I used 7gypsies)

Cardstock for labels

Paper piercer

Basic grey bookplates

Brads

Ribbon of your choice

Chalk ink

Scrapbook adhesive
(I used 3L E-Z Runner)

*We all have magazines
or catalogues around the
house or office and we are
always looking for a perfect
storage solution. These
scrapped magazine holders
make a beautiful gift for
any household or office desk.
It will bring order from
clutter and look attractive
in any office or living room.
Use it for magazines, books or
folders, and adjust your labels
accordingly.*

1 Paint the magazine holder in the colour of your choice. Allow to dry thoroughly.

2 Cut the patterned paper into to strips of 11 x 26,5 cm (4.3 x 10.4 in).

3 Tear the edges to fit the tall back end of the magazine holder and adhere to the magazine holder.

4 Print the word *Magazines* or a suitable label for the content of the magazine holder onto cardstock.

5 Place the bookplate over the writing to measure the size and cut the word to fit. Fasten with the brads and stick onto the patterned paper on the magazine holder with adhesive.

6 Finally wrap the ribbon around the magazine holder and tie a bow in front for a beautiful finish.

Photo necklace

YOU WILL NEED

Ultra ShapeXpress™

Circle template

Pliers

Chain of your choice

Knitted flower

Textile flower

Buttons

Ribbon

Felt

Photo

Scrapbook adhesive

Embellishments of your choice

A photo necklace is a wonderful way to keep your family or loved ones close to your heart all day. It will attract a lot of attention and be a true trendsetting project. It makes a quick and easy gift that is sure to be appreciated. Also, make a few for yourself in various colour schemes. I used classic black and white. My chain is long enough to go over my head. If you prefer it shorter, attach a clasp.

1 Cut the chain to the length of your choice, weave the ribbon through the holes of the chain and tie them in a secure knot.

2 Position the flowers on the necklace and secure them with their fasteners or by sewing the flowers onto the ribbon.

3 Using the Ultra ShapeXpress™, cut your photo into a circle, then cut a felt circle slightly larger and glue the photo onto it. Embellish with ribbon and a button, and attach to the chain by sewing the felt onto the ribbon in the chain.

4 If preferred, add further embellishments such as beads, buttons or more flowers.

Desktop noteboard

YOU WILL NEED

Trimmer

Craft mat

Finger craft knife

Flexible stainless steel ruler

Patterned paper

Chipboard

Cardstock

Upper crest border punch
(I used Fiskars)

Ribbon

Tags

Scrapbook adhesive

Embellishments

A desktop noteboard is a lovely gift or scrapbooking idea to brighten up any person's desk and day. It will be used through the year and it is a beautiful way to remind someone of their loved ones and why they work so hard. Embellish it as much or as little as you like, and leave plenty of space for notes, reminder tags, photos, post-its and so on. It will work equally well on a wall.

1 Using the finger craft knife and steel ruler, cut your chipboard to 50 x 60 cm.

2 Chalk the top and outer edges of the patterned paper.

3 Adhere the patterned paper to the top of the chipboard.

4 Use the border punch and punch the top border of both the cardstock pages, taking care to match the sides where they will meet.

5 Glue down securely over the patterned paper, covering the bottom half of the board.

6 Finally, place bands of ribbon around the board to provide a space to attach photos, notes, accounts or letters. You can also personalise the board by permanently adhering a matted photo, as well as any further embellishments you wish.

Photo box

A photo box is a wonderful surprise gift. When the lid is removed and the layers of photos flap open, it never fails to elicit a big "Wow!" Make several for yourself or surprise friends and family with their own special memory boxes. You don't have to fill every space with photos – use some for embellishments or just add your favourite patterned paper.

1 Trim a sheet of cardstock to 30 x 30 cm (11 x 11 in). Cut out a 10 cm (3.9 in) square from each corner. Trim a different colour sheet of cardstock to 27 x 27 cm (10.6 x 10.6 in). Cut a 9 cm (3.5 in) square from each corner. Trim a third sheet, the same colour as the first, to 24 x 24c m (9.4 in) and cut an 8 x 8 cm (3.1 in) square from each corner. These three sheets will form the box.

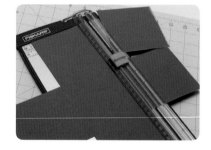

2 Once cutting is completed, score along every section that will be folded.

3 Cut a piece of cardstock to 14 x 14 cm (5.5 x 5.5 in) for the lid. Score a 2 cm (0.8 in) edge all around the square. Cut along the vertical score line up to the horizontal score line at the top and bottom of two opposite sides. Fold over the tabs you have created, and stick down securely onto the remaining sides to shape the lid.

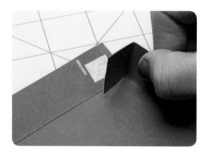

4 Fold and chalk all the edges of the booklet box and the lid.

5 Cut a 9 cm (3.5 in) square from a sheet of patterned paper and adhere to the top of the lid. Take care to position it accurately in the centre of the lid. Decorate further as you wish.

6 Cut two strips of 3,5 cm (1.4 in) from the coordinating sheet of patterned paper, and trim these to four 10 cm (3.9) sections. Adhere these to the outside of the biggest cardstock sheet, halfway down each side, ensuring that they line up perfectly when the sides are folded up.

7 Cut your photographs to size to fit the squares you have created, adhere them as you wish to the squares you have created and decorate with stickers and other embellishments of your choice. Leave the centre square of the two bigger book sections open.

8 Apply adhesive to the wrong side of the centre square of the smallest book section and glue to the right side of the middle section, ensuring accurate placement in the centre. Repeat with the middle section, sticking it to the largest section.

Photo in a tray

YOU WILL NEED

Craft mat

Tray

Round die-cut patterned paper
(I used Pitter Patter Sophie
Flower by Making Memories)

Chalk ink

Sanding block

Photograph

Chipboard alphabet letter

Glimmer mist (I used Dazzles
dye spray by Enmarc in
Pink Flamingo)

Misting mat or newspaper

Dodz adhesive dots

Cardstock circle for title

Brads

Ribbon

Flower

Glitter glue

Scrapbook adhesive
(I used 3L E-Z Runner)

A delicate dove-grey serving tray was the inspiration for this magical vintage wall hanging or display counter piece. The scalloped cardstock adds to the soft, feminine look and glimmer mist on the lettering creates even more magic. The beautiful photo remains the centre piece.

1 Chalk the edges of the die-cut patterned paper.

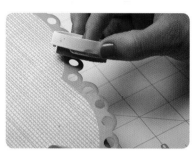

2 Sand the edges of your photo to enhance the vintage look.

3 Adhere the photo to the die-cut patterned paper, then glue them onto the tray using scrapbooking adhesive.

4 Using the glimmer mist and misting mat (or an old newspaper), spray the alphabet letter. Pat dry with a kitchen towel to remove excess spray and allow to dry.

5 Stick a flower onto the alphabet letter using Dodz, then adhere the alphabet letter to the photo.

6 Chalk the edge of the cardstock circle and write the title in ink and glitter glue.

7 Add further embellishments as you prefer.

Coffee mug shot

YOU WILL NEED

Re-usable coffee mug with removable sleeve

Trimmer

Craft mat

Patterned paper
(I used Heidi Grace)

Scissors

Chalk ink

Photos

Stickers (I used Heidi Grace)

Rub-ons

Scrapbook adhesives
(I used 3L E-Z Runner)

Pencil

1 Remove the current sleeve inner of the coffee mug and use it as a template to transfer the shape to your choice of patterned paper. Cut out.

2 Chalk the edges of the paper shape.

3 Adhere your photos and embellish with stickers and rub-ons.

4 Position around the cup and return the plastic outer sleeve. You could also place a special message in the cup to be read when the recipient opens the gift.

This was one of my husband's all time favourite gifts. I made it for him as part of a series of birthday gifts and he still uses it every day. You could give this to your mom, dad, husband, friend, children, anybody who travels regularly or is off to school. The recipient will be reminded of you daily and appreciate the beautiful crafts you have made. These mugs are readily available from homeware stores.

Photo multi-frame

Photo frames of all shapes and sizes are so easy to come by nowadays and are available from homeware stores, camera shops and stationers, among others. I simply printed my photographs all the same size and placed them in the multi-frame guides, then added rub-ons, lettering and other embellishments to create a scrapbook page in a frame, ready to display on the wall.

1 Remove the glass and inner guide from the photo frame.

2 Trim your photos to fit the openings in the frame and arrange them in a pleasing sequence.

3 Adhere the photos in position using scrapbook adhesive and add words and motifs using rub-ons. I used one opening for my title – chipboard letters glued to cardstock. I inked the edges of the cardstock before positioning it in the inner frame.

4 Replace the glass and backing of the frame and attach the threaded beads.

5 To form the date, chalk the edges of the numerals, cover with dimensional glue and allow to dry thoroughly. Open the wire rings, connect the numerals in the right order and close using the pliers. Finally attach to the photoframe.

all yours

love

DUBAI

Tea tray treat

I love making serving trays like this for family and friends for their birthdays. The tray is exactly the right size so you can scrapbook one 30 x 30 cm (12 x 12 in) page and simply place it in the tray. I lay a glass sheet over the embellished page to ensure that the decoration is durable. In this way you can also change the decoration regularly to give the tray a fresh look and feel.

1 Paint the tray, allowing it to dry thoroughly between coats. Dry-brush the sides of the tray to give it a distressed look. You could also create a distressed look by applying a darker coat of paint over a lighter one and then lightly sanding it when dry.

2 Chalk the edges of the patterned paper that will be your background.

3 Cut four groups of circles of 7.5 cm (3 in), 6 cm (2.4 in), 5 cm (2 in), 2,5 cm (1 in) and 2 cm (0.8 in), alternating between two different coordinating sheets of patterned paper.

4 Chalk the edges of all the circles and fold as shown in the photo.

5 Pierce each circle in the centre, assemble them in various arrangements to form flowers, and adhere them to the background paper using a brad. Arrange them in a pleasing combination.

6 Prepare the lettering for your title and adhere it in a suitable position.

7 Outline selected sections of the background pattern with dimensional glue to add interest and texture.

8 Allow to dry thoroughly, place in the tray and cover with the clear glass. Tie several ribbons to the tray handles for a pretty finishing touch.

TEA for two

Heart cushion banner

YOU WILL NEED

Ultra ShapeXpress™ and
heart template

Beading chain (about 1 m)

Ribbon (about 1,2 m)

Craft mat

2 striped fabric heart cushions

Light brown cardstock

Flexible wire

Pliers

Eyelets

Eyelet-setting tool

Patterned paper

Decorative pins
(I used Heidi Grace)

Scrapbook adhesive

Chalk

Brads

Photos (6)

Paperclips

Flexible wire

Lace

Other embellishments

*Gingham and stripes excite
me – hence the inspiration
for this gorgeous heart cushion
banner. This makes a lovely
gift for a baby's christening or
naming ceremony, and becomes
an appreciated memento.*

1 Thread the ribbon through
the chain.

2 Cut three hearts each
from two different sheets of
patterned paper using the
Ultra ShapeXpress™ and heart
template. Insert eyelets into the
tops of these hearts, as well as
the fabric hearts. Chalk the edges
of the paper hearts.

3 Print the title of your project on
the cardstock and cut it out using
the Ultra ShapeXpress™ and heart
template. Chalk the edges and
decorate with brads.

4 Adhere to one of the fabric
hearts using a decorative pin.

5 Cut six photos out with the
Ultra ShapeXpress™ and adhere
these to the patterned paper hearts
using paper clips.

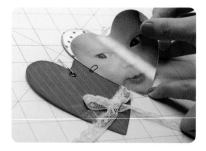

6 Attach the fabric hearts to
the ends of the chain using the
flexible wire and pliers, then
space the remaining hearts
evenly and attach. Add further
embellishments in the form of
ribbons, lace, rub-ons or whatever
you prefer.

Memory bag

YOU WILL NEED

Trimmer
Craft mat
Punches (I used Fiskars upper crest border punch and Fiskars Lever punch for scalloped circles)
Plastic bag with side pockets (I bought mine at Nataniël's Kaalkop shop)
Ruler
2 sheets of cardstock
4 sheets of patterned paper (I used Heidi Swapp)
Chalk
Lettering of choice
Small stapler
Ribbon, buttons and embellishments of choice
Scrapbooking adhesive

Every woman needs a bag, whether it's a handbag, a beach bag or just a magazine holder. A sling bag with transparent side pockets can be a window on your world if you dolly it up with scrapbook techniques, using a striking combination of paper, photos and other embellishments. And whenever you want a new look, you can simply replace these.

1 Count and measure the side pockets of the bag.

2 Cut cardstock and patterned paper to these sizes, each as background for half the number of pockets. Chalk some, or all, of them.

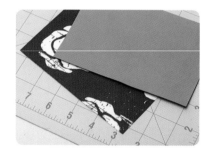

3 Punch scalloped circles and/or other shapes from the remaining patterned paper, chalk and place randomly on the backgrounds. I also finished the edges of smaller pieces of patterned paper with the upper crest border punch and stapled them to chalked cardstock for variety.

4 Adhere photos and embellishments to the backgrounds and glue down your lettering, if used.

5 Finally tie the ribbon in a beautiful bow around one of the slings of the bag.

Wooden spool photo holders

YOU WILL NEED

Craft mat

Wooden ribbon spools
(I bought mine from www.
ebonyandivoryribbons.co.za)

Patterned paper

Circle punches or template
(2 sizes)

Chalk

Photos (post-card size,
matted and chalked)

Self-adhesive clear overlays
with border frame
(to fit size of matted photos)

Photo holders

Ribbon

Scrapbook adhesive

1 Cut or punch two small and two larger circles from the patterned paper to embellish the tops of the spools. Chalk them, adhere the smaller circle to the bigger one, and stick to the tops of the spools.

2 Wind the ribbon neatly around the spools.

3 Make a hole in the centre of each spool by drilling or using a small nail and hammer. Place the photo holders into these holes.

4 Cover the matted and chalked photographs with the self-adhesive border overlays. This adds a final touch to your photos and protects them.

5 Add your photos to the photo holders and wait for the compliments to roll in.

I absolutely adore ribbon, especially if it is neatly packed, stacked or twirled. I love the texture and many application possibilities. This project was born from my love for ribbon. When I saw these wooden spools online, I simply could not resist them! They make eye-catching and unusual photo holders, created in a jiffy. To change the look of your photo holders, simply change the ribbon.

Initialled frame

1 If the frame has a glass front, remove it and paint the frame and the initial in contrasting colours. Allow to dry.

2 Dry-brush the initial using the second colour and allow to dry completely.

3 Measure the inside of the frame and cut the flocked patterned paper to siz; replace the glass. If you are using photos, position, embellish and adhere these before fitting the glass in the frame.

4 Glue the painted initial to the outside of the frame using wood glue.

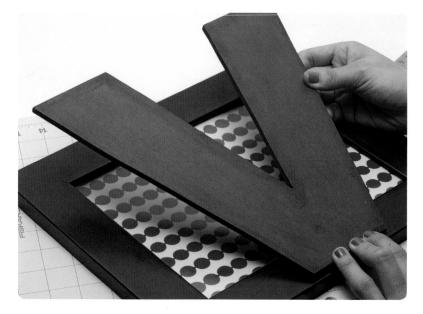

Initials are widely used in interior decor nowadays, and combining their use with scrapbooking techniques seemed just natural. This framed initial can be further personalised by using photos in the frame behind the initial, or even on the initial. I really liked the textured paper and my mini easel provided the ideal display solution.

Initialled printer's tray

Printer's trays are just so versatile. When decorating my new studio I decided to make another one, working around the initial J. While J is my initial, in this instance it refers to the word journey, signifying my own journey and the significant role of my home and my studio.

1 Paint the printer's tray brown and allow to dry. Dry-brush the sides and panelling using the cream paint.

2 Measure the blocks of the printer's tray and cut the patterned paper to these sizes. Chalk them if preferred.

3 Print the title *Home is where your journey begins* (or what you have chosen as your title) on the cardstock and cut it out smaller than one of the blocks. Mat this onto a different colour cardstock leaving a 5 mm frame, and adhere to the patterned paper for the block you have chosen.

4 Embellish the other patterned paper blocks using stickers and the chipboard letter, and adhere to the various sections of the printer's tray.

5 Glue the word *home* or a word of your choice to the top edge over two panels to reinforce the 3D effect of the printer's tray.

6 Using the Ultra ShapeXpress™ and butterfly template, cut a butterfly from the remaining patterned paper.

7 Thread the ribbon through the bead, adhere the ribbon to the butterfly and attach this assembly to the bottom of the printer's tray.

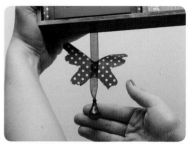

Vintage baking recipes

YOU WILL NEED

Trimmer

Craft mat

13 x 22 cm (5.1 x 8.7 in)
ring-bound mini book

12 sheets of patterned paper

Ruler

Chipboard letters

Craft knife

Sanding block

Paint

Paintbrushes

Gaffer tape

Letter sheet

Binder punch

Tags

Ribbon and other
embellishments

Chalk

Recipes (printed or hand-
written on separate sheets of
paper, envelopes or tags)

Scrapbook adhesive

This recipe book was inspired by my love of baking. I also adore the vintage look, so the paper, mini book, gaffer tape and embellishments from 7gypsies were just perfect. Compiling your own mini book is a great way to preserve memorable recipes and always have them on hand.

1 Remove the spine from the mini book pages, measure them and cut your patterned papers to size. Glue the patterned paper to the mini book pages.

2 Punch holes in the pages, using a suitable binder punch, so you can bind the book again once your pages are completed.

3 Prepare your book and section titles by painting some and covering others in patterned paper. For the latter, apply adhesive to the front of the lettering and lay face down on the back of the patterned paper. Cut out neatly and lightly sand the edges. Painted lettering can either be dry-brushed with a darker or lighter colour, or also lightly sanded.

4 Adhere your book and section titles to the pages and embellish with buttons, ribbons, brads and whatever you prefer.

5 Glue your printed recipes to the pattern pages and embellish.

6 Continue this process until you are happy with your pages, then re-assemble the book by placing the pages back into the spine.

Creative clipboards

Clipboards represent serious tasks and to do lists – checking and ticking off information for tasks to be completed. I decided to make a not-so-serious clipboard project that can be used decoratively as well as functionally. Label five decorated clipboards from Monday to Friday and hang them on your wall to enjoy, or for creative to-do lists.

I Measure the width of the clipboards and trim several sheets of patterned paper to size. Chalk and/or tear some edges.

2 Trim cardstock to the width of the clipboards and about 10 cm (4 in) deep. Adhere the cardstock to the top of the clipboards, pushing it as far up as it would go when you lift the clip.

3 Print the titles (Monday to Friday) on paper and tear out. Chalk the edges and glue to the cardstock.

4 Adhere the patterned paper to the open areas of the clipboards, either just one sheet or various sheets in differing heights.

5 Turn over and cut around the corners using the craft knife.

6 Cover the space above the clamp with gaffer tape and trim the corners.

7 Create pockets for storing notes, reminders, invoices and so on by trimming a sheet of paper to well over half the size of the clipboard. Tear and chalk the top edge if you prefer and turn over a flap of about 2,5 cm. Adhere the sides and bottom to the clipboard, leaving the top free to slip in items.

8 Add further embellishments including stamping, more paper strips, cord and string to attach notes with clips, as well as mini envelopes left open at the top.

Baby keepsake box

YOU WILL NEED

Trimmer with scoring blade

Craft mat

Wooden box with lid windows
(I found this one ready
painted and distressed)

2 sheets of patterned paper

1 sheet of cardstock

Photo

Chalk

Sparkles or gems

Chipboard lettering

Sanding block

Keepsakes

Ranger stickles

Scrapbook adhesive

Metal ruler

Chalk

Ribbon

Tag

It is always a delight to create scrapbooking items for babies. While working on these items I think of new life, new beginnings and happy memories. This box is meant to store a collection of small keepsakes of a new bundle of joy – include any small items as a reminder.

1 Measure the lid windows and cut three pieces of the same patterned paper to size, chalk them and adhere to the wooden backing.

2 Add your photo to the middle block. Embellish it with some sparkles or gems (I used Heidi Swapp).

3 Sand the chipboard letters with the sanding block to create a distressed look, tear a piece of patterned paper to size, chalk it and adhere the title. Now adhere this to the box, above the lid's hinges.

4 Measure the inside bottom and back of the lid, cut patterned paper (preferably two different designs) to size and adhere.

5 Make a small mini book by cutting the cardstock 28 x 6 cm (11 x 2.4 in). Use a scoring blade and score the strip every 7 cm (2.8 in); fold on the score lines. Chalk the edges and jot down your favourite memories of, or keepsake words for, the baby. Decorate with stickles and rub-ons or whatever you prefer. Tie with a ribbon and place in the keepsake box together with booties, a bib and your other keepsakes.

6 Wrap the ribbon around the box several times and secure with the tag.

Envelope album

I got this idea from Cheryl, a fellow Fisk-a-teer – thank you Cheryl! It is a hit and quite easy to make. You simply stick together several envelopes and decorate them with patterned paper and embellishments to make a mini album. Fill the envelopes with vouchers, photos and keepsakes, and you have gift of note! I used metal wording for the title Create, *and filled the envelopes with gift vouchers from craft shops.*

I Open the flaps of the envelopes and adhere the flap of one to the bottom front of the next until you have joined them all together. Work neatly and use a good adhesive that will not leave marks on the envelopes.

2 Embellish the envelopes with pieces of patterned paper, die cuts, ribbon, rub-ons, shapes and so on to tell your story. Adhere the title and other embellishments to the top envelope that will form the front of the album.

3 Measure the envelope and trim cardstock to size to fit into each envelope. Chalk the edges of the cardstock and slip into the envelopes to strengthen your album. If preferred, you can also scrap each piece of cardstock with photos, patterned paper and other memorabilia.

4 Cut a suitably sized slit into the flap of the top envelope and weave through a length of ribbon. Wrap the ribbon around the envelopes and tie into a beautiful bow.

Mini pocket-envelope album

I absolutely adore any mini tags, envelopes, cards, books or diaries, hence my inspiration to create an album using mini pocket envelopes and tags. (A pocket envelope has a flap on a short side instead of a long one.) It's easy and fun to do. You can follow my instructions or just do your own thing.

1 Lay out the envelopes in two rows to plan the placement of your embellishments before using any adhesive.

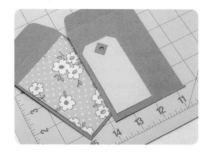

2 Chalk all the envelopes all around – including the flap at the top.

3 Cut two cork rectangles slightly smaller than the envelopes, as well as a scalloped strip and place them on three envelopes.

4 Cut out a cork butterfly, using the Ultra ShapeXpress™ and butterfly template. I used this for the front of my mini album.

5 Place a parcel or clothing tag on every second envelope.

6 Cut patterned paper to size and place on selected envelopes, then distribute ribbon, buttons and other embellishments between all the envelopes to decorate them, chalking edges as you go along before adhering.

7 Cut five squares of 5 cm (2 in) from patterned paper. Score them in the middle using your trimmer and scoring blade. Fold on the score line and round the corners at the fold with your corner rounder.

8 Chalk the edges of the tabs and adhere a tab to every second envelope.

9 Wrap a ribbon around the envelopes and tie together with a neat bow.

Dog treat jars

YOU WILL NEED

Trimmer

Craft mat

Circle punch

Tag punch

3 glass jars

Ribbon

1 sheet patterned paper

1 sheet cardstock

3 photos of dogs, matted onto cardstock

Chalk ink

Brads

Scrapbook adhesive

Dodz adhesive dots

Dog treats

1 Thoroughly clean and dry the glass jars and fill with treats.

2 Punch three circles from the patterned paper to fit the lids of the jars. Chalk the circles and adhere them to the tops of the lids.

3 Wrap ribbon around the necks of the jars, finishing with a good sized bow.

4 Punch three tags from cardstock. Chalk them and write descriptions or the names of the dogs on the tags. Attach to the ribbon using brads.

5 Finally add the photographs, attaching them with Dodz.

Dogs are man's best friend and to some they are their children – including my neighbour and her precious K9 kids. I wanted to make her a special thank you gift for being a wonderful friend and confidante and I knew a treat for her dogs would be a treat for her. I decorated empty coffee jars (Douwe Egbert – the coffee is really lovely too!) filled them with treats and added photos of her beloved dachshunds.

Framed jewellery

YOU WILL NEED

Craft mat

Oval frame

Sandpaper

Paint (2 contrasting colours, light and dark)

Crack medium

Paintbrush

Felt

Staple gun

Craft knife

Clear accents with borders (I used Heidi Grace)

Title label

Brads

Scrapbook adhesive

1 Thoroughly sand the frame and wipe away any dust and dirt. Cover with a coat of darker paint and allow to dry. Apply crack medium with your brush strokes going in the same direction and leave to dry. Finish off with a coat of light paint, using the same brush strokes as before, and leave to dry for at least two hours to allow cracks to form.

2 Attach the felt to the back of the frame using a staple gun, pulling it tight to fit. Carefully cut away the excess felt using a craft knife.

3 Reinforce the felt backing by adding more staples.

4 Embellish the felt inside with clear accents and attach the title using brads. Jewellery such as earrings can be inserted into the clear accents, while brooches have their own pins to hook onto the felt. Decorative pins will also work as well as enhance your display.

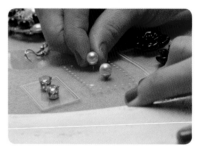

Frames are delightful and versatile items – they can host the obvious photos or you could recycle them to do much more. This project shows you how to turn an antique-look frame into a unique jewellery holder, putting both the frame and your favourite costume jewellery on display.

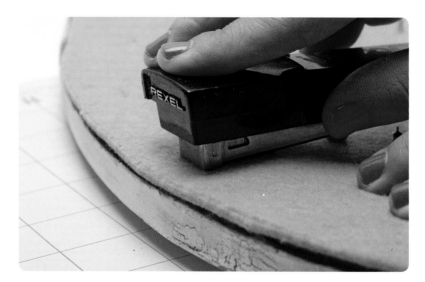

Felt mini book

YOU WILL NEED

Trimmer

Craft mat

Grey and turquoise felt

Liquid glue
(I used Tombo Aqua)

Photos

Patterned paper

Metallic chipboard heart
shapes or own choice

Ghost hearts or own choice

Ghost alphabet or own choice

Pexel tool

Chalk

Ribbon

1 Trim the turquoise felt to three pieces of 20 cm x 15 cm (8 x 6 in) and the grey felt to two pieces of 20 cm x 15 cm (8 x 6 in).

2 Place on top of one another, alternating the colours, fold over in the centre and bind the pages with your favourite piece of coordinating ribbon.

3 Trim photos and patterned paper to fit the felt pages. Chalk the edges and adhere in pleasing combinations using adhesive.

4 Add clear accents such as hearts and lettering to embellish the pages and adhere with the Pexel tool and liquid glue.

Felt is such a versatile medium and is used in scrapbooking for mini albums, wording, shapes and so on. This booklet makes a great keepsake that will last a lifetime with its felt basis. The photos and embellishments are adhered with liquid glue, and the pages are easily bound by tying them with a pretty ribbon. I used Heidi Swapp embellishments and lettering.

The list: notebook on canvas

1 Paint the canvas light pink. Leave to dry and dry-brush the sides dark pink.

2 Stamp a border onto the canvas using clear acrylic stamps and craft paint.

3 Use the alphabet stickers to form the title *The list.*

4 Chalk the edges of the notebook and embellish it with brads and stamps.

5 Finally adhere the notebook to the canvas and place in a convenient spot where you will always find it when you need to make lists.

Note taking is an everyday responsibility. Jotting down your notes on beautiful books and papers could make this task much more fun. And to ensure that it is always where you need it, adhere it to a blocked canvas and use it decoratively on your kitchen wall or an interesting stand.

Coffee-cup album

I love coffee and I am an unashamed coffee snob. I have a few favourite blends and I absolutely love Starbucks, especially in their convenient take-away cups! For me coffee is also about sharing time and creating new memories. So what better way to preserve some of these than recycling my take-away Starbucks coffee-cups (of which I have plenty!), into a mini album?

1 Thoroughly rinse and dry the coffee cup and carefully cut out the bottom.

2 Flatten the cup and cut it open along the one fold line. Work neatly as this will be the cover of your album.

3 Use the cofee cup as a template and trace onto five sheets of cardstock. Cut out and chalk all the edges, including those of the coffee cup cover.

4 Adhere a cardstock shape to the inside of the coffee cup to reinforce it.

5 Carefully mark the centre of each coffee cup shape, score from top to bottom, fold and assemble your book. Adhere your photos and embellishments to all the other cardstock shapes, using both sides. Using your alphabet letters stick down titles for each photo.

6 Punch holes through all the pages about 2,5 cm (3 in) from each edge in the centre and thread ribbon through the holes to bind the album.

Butterfly mobile

*Special décor projects for babies
and children are always a
treat – for me more so if I can
do them in pink! This mobile
is so easy to assemble and
can be completed in about an
hour. You can be sure that it
will brighten up any baby or
little girl's room. I used only
butterflies and acrylic beads*

1 Separate the inner and outer
embroidery rings and spray
paint, including the screw. Allow
to dry.

2 Using the template, cut eight
large and eight smaller butterflies
from the patterned paper and
chalk all the edges.

3 Cut eight lengths of satin and
organza ribbon, thread a bead
through one end of each length
and tie to secure.

4 Score all the butterflies down
the centre and attach along the
score line in pairs, combining
different patterns. Fold the upper
butterflies along the score line
so their wings will stand up, and
attach the butterflies to the satin
ribbon using liquid glue.

5 Tie all the ribbons to the outer
ring of the embroidery hoop,
alternating satin and organza,
evenly spaced, before replacing
the inner ring and tightening
the screw.

6 Finally, twirl together three
equal lengths of satin, organza
and patterned ribbon to form the
top hanger. Attach in three evenly
spaced positions on the embroidery
hoop and gather at the top.
Ensure that the mobile is perfectly
balanced before tying the ribbons
in a loop from which the mobile
can be suspended.

Denim pocket album

Everybody wears denims and there will always be a pair of discarded denims lying around. Now you can save the pockets and put them to good use. This denim pocket mini album is a fun project, especially for children. Just make sure that they don't cut up their new denims!

1 Carefully remove the pockets from a discarded pair of denim jeans and trace the outline of the pocket onto chipboard, cardstock and patterned paper.

2 Using the craft knife cut out four chipboard pockets and paint the sides.

3 Adhere the denim pockets to two chipboard pockets, forming the front and back covers of your album, and patterned paper to both sides of the remaining two as inner pages of the album.

4 Cover a chipboard flower with patterned paper and use as an accent for the cover.

5 Embellish the front cover by cutting a cardstock and patterned paper pocket and partly adhering it to insert journalling or further embellishments.

6 Add the title using chipboard lettering and a printed or handwritten label.

7 Fill your album with photos, mementoes, embellishments and whatever you may wish. Use cardstock cut to the template for further inserts and fill with photos.

8 Bind by punching a hole in each pocket's top left hand corner and bind with a binder ring. Finish of with beautiful ribbons tied onto the binder ring.

Love canvas

YOU WILL NEED

Trimmer

Craft mat

2 blocked canvases of
the same size

Craft paint (dark and
light brown)

Sponge applicator

2 sheets of patterned paper
with wording (I used 7gypsies
love and *friends*)

Ribbon

Buttons and string

Large chipboard letters

Chipboard words

Chipboard cutouts

Liquid glue

Chalk

Photos

Embellishments

Scrapbook adhesive

Canvas is a very versatile medium. I made this project for our bedroom as a reminder of our love. I used the same photo on both canvases, changing the composition on the second canvas slightly to keep it interesting, but similar enough to symbolise togetherness.

1 Paint the canvases dark brown and allow to dry. If the finish is streaky it doesn't matter as this will just add interesting texture. Dry-brush the edges with the light brown paint and allow to dry.

2 Paint the chipboard letters light brown and dry-brush with dark brown. Allow to dry and adhere to the two canvases. I placed mine aligned to the right.

3 Fill the rest of the canvases with your photos and patterned paper cut to the desired sizes, as well as tags, embellishments, ribbons and words. Chalk the edges of paper and photos to add interest. I used ribbon on both canvases to create continuity. Adhere the patterned paper and photos to the canvas over the ribbon. Paint the chipboard cutouts, allow to dry, and attach using liquid glue.

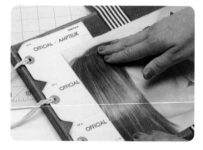

4 Thread a selection of matching buttons onto thin string, arranged from large to small, and attach to the bottom of the canvas as a quirky finishing touch.

Wooden anniversary frame

YOU WILL NEED

Trimmer
Craft mat
Partitioned antique frame, painted
Sandpaper
Chipboard letters for your title (I used *eight*)
Paint and applicator for chipboard
Rub-on words to suit the theme
Bone folder
Chalk
Scrapbook adhesive
Photos
Cardstock

1 Lightly sand the edges of the frame to create a distressed look.

2 Paint the chipboard letters and allow to dry. Use the bone folder to apply the rub-on words to the letters.

3 Trim white cardstock to size, adhere the letters to form the word eight and place into the bottom left section of the rame.

4 Print a special message on pink cardstock, trim to size and place in the top right section.

5 Trim your photos to size, adhere to cardstock and place in the remaining sections.

I found this interesting antique frame with its useful hooks at a pawn shop, covered in dust. I just knew that I would be able to put it to good use, and it was the ideal base for a special eighth wedding anniversary present for my husband. I had the photos printed in black and white with a magenta tint, with my dress and my husband's flower in colour. This frame would also make for a great display of family portraits.

Cutesy key holder

YOU WILL NEED

Trimmer
Craft mat
Wooden frame
Crafters paint for wood
Metal hooks (enough for your title)
Chipboard letters for your title
Hand punch
Chalk
Photo
Patterned paper
Textile flowers with brads
Flower rub-on
Ribbon
Scrapbook adhesive

A key holder is an essential household item but that does not mean that it has to be boring. By using a scrapbooked frame with hooks, you can turn it into a gorgeous display piece – easily changed or updated when the time is right. I used a photo of my most favourite twins in the world, Amy and Zoe.

1 Screw the metal hooks into the bottom of the frame, evenly spaced, and paint the frame the desired colour. Allow to dry thoroughly.

2 Trim a sheet of patterned paper to size to fit the frame and chalk the edges.

3 Trim your photo smaller than this all round and chalk the edges, then adhere to the patterned paper. Embellish with a textile flower and a flower rub-on.

4 Adhere more flowers to the frame then insert the matted photo into the frame and stick down.

5 Punch holes into the letters using the hand punch and hang them on the metal hooks to form the title.

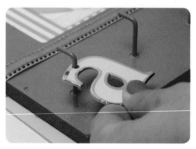

6 Wrap a length of ribbon around the frame and tie it in a beautiful bow to finish off.

Pizza pan babies

YOU WILL NEED

Trimmer
Craft mat
Ruler
Scissors
3 mini pizza pans
Paint and applicator
3 photos 10 x 15 cm (4 x 6 in)
Ultra ShapeXpress™ and super-sized circle template
3 sheets cardstock (one light, two bright pink)
Ribbon
Chalk
Scrapbook adhesive
Eyelet and eyelet setter

1 Thoroughly clean the pizza pans and dry-brush the edges to add definition.

2 Using the Ultra ShapeXpress™ and super sized circle template circles cut three circles of 11,5 cm (4.5 in) from the bright pink cardstock. Repeat this with the photos, adhere the photos to the cardstock circles, then place into the pizza pans and glue down.

3 Print the babies' names on light pink cardstock and trim to 8 x 16 cm (3.1 x 6.2 in) strips.

4 Set an eyelet in the middle of the tag.

5 Chalk all the edges, thread the ribbon through the eyelet and tie to the pizza pans with a pretty bow.

When my dear friend recently welcomed her two beautiful girls into this world she called them Amy and Zoe and they soon became the A to Z of our lives, like their names indicate. They have completely filled our lives with love and laughter. I did not think their mom would mind if I captured them in a set of small pizza pans to adorn her kitchen wall.

Memory hanger

YOU WILL NEED

Trimmer

Craft mat

Ultra ShapeXpress™ and heart template

Wire hanger

Paint and applicator

Ribbon

Wax cord

Beads

Chipboard butterflies

Hand punch

Cardstock

Photos

Chalk

Flowers, lace and other embellishments

Selection of clips

Scrapbook adhesive

Wire hangers are useful tools beyond bringing your dry cleaning home and opening the car when you've locked your keys inside (before the advent of central locking …). When I saw this pretty heart hanger, I could think of nothing better than to use it as a love memory keepsake. By changing the colouring and attachments, you could easily turn this into a baby mobile.

1 Paint the hanger the desired colour and allow to dry.

2 Use the Ultra ShapeXpress™ and heart template and cut cardstock and photos into hearts of various sizes. Chalk all the edges and embellish the cardstock hearts with rub-ons, stickers and lace, or whatever you prefer.

3 Cut a length of wax cord to 75 cm (30 in). Punch holes in the butterflies and thread the beads and the butterflies onto the wax cord, using knots to space them at regular intervals.

4 Cut the ribbon into six lengths of 75 cm (30 in) and adhere the photo hearts, cardstock hearts, flowers, lace and other embellishments using various clips.

5 Tie the wax cord in the centre of the hanger and add the ribbon, three on each side, evenly spaced.

6 Finish with a big heart and a corded bead at the top and hang on a wall or door.

Vintage frame note-holder

YOU WILL NEED

Craft mat

Vintage frame

Sandpaper

Spray paint

Craft paint and applicator

Small screw-in hooks

Wax cord

Chipboard letters

Glimmer mist (I used Dazzles)

Small tea doilies

Wire words

Clips

Chalk

Ribbon

Embellishments

Scrapbook adhesive

My father-in-law gave me this lovely old frame. It must date back many years ago and I could not wait to turn it into a useful, everyday item. I spray painted it (pink, of course!), strung cord from side to side, added a selection of clips and Voila! – I now have a fun and striking note holder.

1 Sand the frame and spray paint. Leave to dry, then dry-brush with white. Turn over and screw the hooks to the back on both sides of the frame at varying heights.

2 Spray the tea doilies with glimmer mist to create a colourful and shimmering embellishment. Leave to dry.

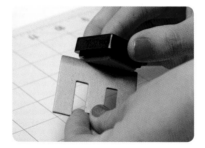

3 Chalk the chipboard letters, then spray them with glimmer mist and leave to dry.

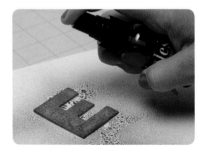

4 Weave the wax cord through the hooks to form a continuous zig-zag from top to bottom.

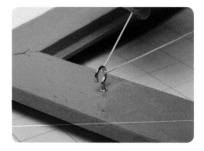

5 Clip on the letters to form the word NOTES and add the painted tea doilies and wire words.

6 Add further embellishments, tags and clips for notes, then tie the ribbon in a bow and adhere to the frame.

Acrylic baby album

YOU WILL NEED

Trimmer
Craft mat
15 x 15 cm (6 x 6 in) acrylic mini album
Patterned paper (I used Heidi Grace)
Hand punch
Cardstock
Sticker letters (I used Heidi Grace)
Scrapbook adhesive (preferably clear drying)
Chipboard letters
Stickle rhinestones
Rub-ons
Embellishments
Ribbon
Buttons
Brads
Photos
Chalk

Acrylic is a wonderful medium to scrapbook because it is transparent, lending itself to unusual effects and finishes. The fact that the pages are transparent also brings with it special challenges and you have to bear in mind that both sides of everything you use will be visible.

1 This album is about baby Karl, so I used a lovely big, bright patterned K on a decorated chipboard circle as my front page. These were adhered to the acrylic page, further embellished with stickle rhinestones.

2 Trim the patterned paper to size and punch holes corresponding to those of the acrylic pages.

3 Adhere the acrylic page to the patterned paper, taking care to align the holes.

4 Continue working like this, using your photos and embellishments and adding titles to the various pages.

5 Finally bind the acrylic album with the binder rings provided and tie some ribbon in a bow to finish it off.

Cupcake pan with recipes

YOU WILL NEED

Craft mat

Ultra ShapeXpress™ and circle templates

Scissors

Cupcake pan

Cardstock

Patterned paper

Pencil

Gaffer tape (I used 7gypsies *measurement*)

Ribbon and cup-cake related embellishments

Chalk

Metal label holders

Removable adhesive

Scalloped chipboard circle

Chipboard letters for *yum*

Turn a humble cupcake tin into a value added gift by decorating it and filling the cups with recipes and theme related embellishments. Then, for good measure, bake and decorate at least one scrumptious cup cake to add before handing it over to the lucky recipient. Nothing is adhered to the tin itself, as it will be used afterwards.

1 Trace the tin lining to the back of a sheet of patterned paper and cut out the circles using scissors. Round the corners using a pair of scissors and place in the tray.

2 Type your recipes in sections that will fit into the size of the circle and print. Using the Ultra ShapeXpress™ and circle template, cut out the printed recipe circles.

3 Chalk the edges of the circles and adhere the recipes with gaffer tape so you will have a booklet for each recipe.

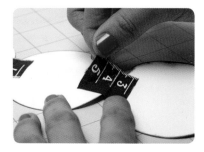

4 Print the words *chocolate* and *cupcake* on cardstock and trim to fit the label holders. Assemble and adhere to the cup cake tin with removable adhesive.

5 Place the recipe booklets in the holes and add further cupcake related embellishments.

6 Finally bake a delicious cupcake using the actual recipe and give it to someone special.

Chocolate Cupcake Recipe
Ingredients
• 2 cups flour
• 2 cups sugar
• 1/2 t baking powder
• t salt
• t baking soda
• 1 cup shortening
• 1/2 cup water
• 1/4 large eggs
• 3/4 cup milk
• teaspoon vanilla
• ounces chocolate

Children's board-book keepsake

Children's board books are always popular and will keep them occupied for hours on end. But what do you do when your child has outgrown the book? Turn it into a special keepsake filled with special photos and memorabilia, creating an entirely new story.

1 Trace the shape of your board book onto patterned paper and cardstock, cut out and cover all the pages of the board book using liquid glue.

2 Allow to dry, then sand and chalk the edges.

3 Stick down a length of gaffer tape on every paper join and trim neatly.

4 Cut your photos into circles using the Ultra ShapeXpress™ and circle template (or whatever shape suits the shape of the book). Chalk the edges, adhere and add embellishments.

5 Adhere the lettering to the book cover, playing with the shape of the book, and add further embellishments.

6 Finally cover the outside spine with gaffer tape and trim.

Thankful mini album

YOU WILL NEED

Trimmer

Craft mat

Ruler

Upper crest border punch

Large circle punch

An A5 lever arch file

2 sheets of patterned paper

2 sheets of cardstock

Embellishments

Clear glue (I used Tombo)

Ribbon

Chalk

Acetate circles (I used
Li'l Davis Designs Foil
Rimmed)

Scrapbook Adhesives

It is very important on a daily, monthly and yearly basis to take stock of the things for which we are thankful. This album was inspired by my overwhelming feelings of gratitude when I reflected on the past year and realized how many special people have crossed my path. I chose five people in my life for whom I am most thankful and I wrote a journal about them.

1 Measure the cover and trim a piece of patterned paper to size, leaving some of the file spine showing if you prefer. Punch a border on one side and chalk all the edges before adhering the paper to the cover.

2 Print your titles and headings, words such as *thankful*, *appreciate* and *thank you*, on cardstock and punch them out using a hand punch.

3 Adhere the acetate circle to the title (thankful) using clear glue, then adhere ribbon to the cover, followed by the title.

4 Print an inside cover page on cardstock, trim to size and chalk the edges. Embellish to your liking (I used a strip of patterned paper – chalked – a button and a heart) and glue in position.

5 Print five *thankful* fillers for the plastic inners, trim and stick onto cardstock cut to size for the inners. Complete the filler pages by adhering a trimmed photograph (chalked) and a few lines of journalling, explaining why you are grateful to have that person in your life. Embellish to taste and slip the completed pages into the plastic inners.

6 Trim plain cardstock to size and adhere to the inside back cover. Embellish with ribbon and glue down another printed circle..

Envelope mini book

*I cannot stop telling you how
enthused I am about mini
books. There are just so many
ways in which to make them –
you can use bought envelopes
of varying sizes, cardstock or
simply patterned paper folded
to form an envelope. This is
how I made this versatile mini
book, using beautiful Heidi
Grace patterned paper.*

1 Trim a sheet of patterned paper
to 27 x 30 cm (10.6 x 11.8 in).

2 Working with the short sides,
score the page at 10 cm (3.9 in)
from the bottom and 8,5 cm (3.3
in) from the top, and fold on the
score lines to form an envelope.
Glue the short sides together and
chalk all the edges.

3 Now score each envelope, facing
right side up, 2 cm (0.8 in) from the
right-hand edge, fold on the score
line and chalk before flattening
it again.

4 Round the corners of the scored
ends with the corner rounder.

5 Punch holes 3 cm (1.2 in) from
the top and bottom and 1 cm (0.4
in) from the left-hand side of each
envelope for threading the ribbon
to bind the book, then bind.

6 Prepare inserts for the envelopes
by trimming the cardstock to 29
x 10 cm (11.4 x 3.9 in). Embellish
by chalking some and embossing
others. These inserts will be used
for photos and journalling.

7 Embellish the envelopes with
ribbon, wording, cut-outs and
whatever you prefer.

8 Finally bind the envelopes to
form a book by threading ribbon
through the holes and making
a bow. Add photos and journal.

Candle box

YOU WILL NEED

Trimmer
Craft mat
Wooden box with lid
Sandpaper
Ruler
Chipboard letters (to spell *candles*)
Craft paint and applicator
Sanding block
2 sheets of patterned paper
1 sheet of cardstock
2 packs of smooth candles
Chalk ink
Ribbon
Scrapbook adhesives
Box of extra-length matches

I find wooden boxes of every shape and size irresistible. They are so versatile and can be recycled again and again. This beautiful box found at a garage sale got a new coat of paint and, with some basic scrapbooking techniques, was turned into a beautiful housewarming gift for friends moving into new home. It was quick and easy to make.

1 Sand the box thoroughly, wipe away all dirt and dust and paint in the colour of your choice. Allow to dry and sand the edges to create a distressed look.

2 Measure the inside of the box and the box lid and cut patterned paper to size.

3 Chalk, then adhere to the bottom of the box as well as the inside of the lid.

4 Print a special message on cardstock and cut out. Glue to the patterned paper lining the lid.

5 Wrap ribbon around each pack of candles and tie with a beautiful bow.

6 Wrap the box of matches with cardstock cut to size and tie with a ribbon. Arrange the candles and matches in the box to fit perfectly.

7 Paint the chipboard letters, allow to dry and chalk the edges. Adhere to the top of the box and finish off by wrapping the box with a satin ribbon, tied in a beautiful bow for a pretty gift presentation.

Fabric-covered mini album

YOU WILL NEED

Trimmer

Craft mat

Craft knife

Ruler

Scalloped circle XL lever punch

Hand-held hole punch

Chipboard

6 sheets patterned paper

2 sheets cardstock

Adhesive-backed fabric (I used Dear Lizzy)

Chalk ink

Embellishments

Ribbon

2 binder rings

Making Memories tool kit

Envelopes

Scrapbook adhesives

I love using new scrapbooking products, so when adhesive-backed fabric came on the scene, I could not wait to use it for a mini album. Incorporating envelopes is a useful way of adding volume and interest to a mini album. They can be embellished, filled with memorabilia and photos or simply decorated.

1 Measure, mark and cut two chipboard squares of 15 cm (5.9 in) for the front and back covers of your mini album.

2 Using the hand-held hole punch, punch a hole 4 cm (1.6 in) from the top, and then bottom of each chipboard square on one side, 1 cm (0.8 in) in from the edge so the binder rings can fit through when you bind the album.

3 Adhere the adhesive-backed fabric to the front and back chipboard covers of your mini album.

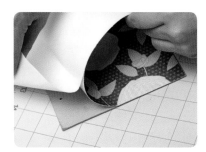

4 Cut as many 15 cm (5.9 in) squares of patterned paper as you like to form the inside pages of the album.

5 Trim cardstock to 8 x 10 cm (3.1 x 3.9 in) rectangles, round the corners and then chalk and adhere to some sheets of patterned paper to serve as journaling blocks.

6 If you prefer, add envelopes to your album. Decorate them by simply punching a scalloped circle to adhere to the flap or use textile flowers or other embellishments.

7 Punch holes into all the pages, chalk the edges and bind the album by fitting the binder rings through the holes. You can either fill the album, or use it as a special gift.

Rolled flower necklace

The collar necklace is one of the latest trends in crafting, so I attempted this project with great enthusiasm. I was very happy with the result and it never fails to draw compliments when I wear it. I have stopped counting how many I have made for friends. And the cherry on top: although you work with fabric, you need absolutely no sewing skills! These flowers can also be used as embellishments for other projects.

1 Use the Ultra ShapeXpress™ and cut three circles from the white felt.

2 Tear or cut the chiffon into strips of 10 cm wide and make a knot at one end.

3 Place a generous dab of glue in the centre of a felt circle, press the knot end of a chiffon strip into the glue, holding it in position with the thumb of one hand.

4 Start twisting and rolling the chiffon with the other hand, adding more glue as you go along to form a flower. Work over the frayed ends to hide them. Set aside to dry and repeat with the other chiffon strips.

5 Arrange the completed flowers in a pleasing shape on the remaining felt, draw sround the outline, cut out and adhere the flowers to the felt.

6 Attach the cord to the flowers by hooking the jumprings into the felt, using the pliers.

Leftover mini book

Every scrapbooker has off-cuts and leftover paper, cardstock and embellishments from other projects. I decided to turn some of mine into a project by delving into my drawer filled with discarded supplies, old cardstock and other bits and pieces. It was great fun trying to put everything to good use, and resulted in a mini book I can now give a crafting friends to fill with memories and treasures. I happened to have an oversupply of pink cardstock which I used as the base. Use whatever you have.

1 Print the title *I love to craft* on cardstock to serve as a front cover and trim to 13 x 21 cm (5.1 x 8.3 in).

2 Strengthen the binding edge with gaffer tape and punch holes for the binder rings 4 cm from the top and bottom and 1 cm inward.

3 Cut several more cardstock pages for the rest of the book and punch holes for the binder rings.

4 Print words and titles onto patterned paper and punch out. Chalk and adhere to selected cardstock pages.

5 Trim patterned paper smaller than the cardstock pages, chalk the edges and adhere to selected pages. Add punched, scalloped circles, chalked and finished with buttons, ribbon and whatever your heart desires.

6 Continue until you have the desired number of pages and bind the book by slipping the binder rings through the holes.

Family clipboard

YOU WILL NEED

Trimmer
Craft mat
White-washed clipboard of 30 x 22 cm (12 x 9.8 in)
Scalloped circle punch
Corner punch
1 sheet cardstock
3 sheets patterned paper
Corrugated cardstock
Dimensional gel
Chipboard letters for your title
Ribbon and other embellishments
Distress ink (I used Tim Holtz vintage photo)
Ink-blending tool
Chalk
Scrapbook adhesive
Photo

Clipboards are versatile and can bring order to your life in many ways. But decorated and given some paper and colour, they become treasures to fill empty spaces on your walls. I used a white-washed clipboard in landscape format bought from a craft shop.

1 Apply distress ink around the edges of the clipboard using the ink blending tool.

2 Apply distress ink to all the chipboard letters in the same way, but cover the entire letter, not just the edges.

3 Outline and fill all the letters with dimensional gel and set aside to allow them to dry completely.

4 Trim a sheet of patterned paper to 29 x 20,5 cm (11.4 x 8.1 in) and round the corners. Chalk all the edges and adhere to the centre of the clipboard.

5 Adhere two more pieces of patterned paper one trimmed to 19 x 11 cm (7.5 x 4.3 in) and the other 18 x 20,5 cm (7.1 x 8.1 in). Chalk the edges before positioning it over the background paper.

6 Trim the corrugated card to 12 x 18 cm (4.7 x 7.1 in). Using the blending tool and distress ink, apply ink lightly all over the woven pattern and glue to the clipboard.

7 Finally add your photo, title and embellishments to the clipboard and hang on your wall.

Flat tin album

You can turn any tin of any form or shape into a delightful gift. This Work in progress is for a friend who can use it for bright and cheerful reminder notes, or to scrap specific memories or simple journalling, or to keep special messages for loved ones.

1 Cut two pieces of cardstock 14 x 12 cm (5.5 x 4.7 in), round the corners, chalk the edges and adhere to the outside top and bottom of the tin.

2 Repeat for the inside top and bottom, using cardstock and patterned paper. Decorate with paper scraps and gaffer tape, and add rub-on wording before adhering to the tin.

3 Cut note cards 13,5 x 11,5 cm (5.3 x 4.5 in) from the remaining cardstock, round the corners and chalk the edges. Cut strips and blocks of patterned paper, chalk the edges and adhere to the note cards. Add rub-on lettering and other embellishments if you prefer.

4 Embellish the top of the tin with patterned paper and the title tag. Use rub-ons to apply the title.

5 Place the note cards in the tin, wrap with your favourite ribbon and tie with a bow.

Mini wedding album

Weddings are the beginning of new relationships, time to catch up on ones that have been neglected and a great reason for scrapbooking. This mini album of my mom's wedding is really special.

1 Cut a chipboard front and back to measure 20 x 12,5 cm (4.9 x 4.9 in). Punch holes in one side, about 2 cm (0.8 in) from the top and bottom, and cut an isosceles triangle of 7,5 cm (3 in) from the other side.

2 Cover with patterned paper and ink the edges. Prepare the title lettering with distress ink and dimensional gel, allow to dry thoroughly and adhere to the front cover.

3 Cut eight pieces of patterned paper 20 x 12 cm (7.9 x 4.7 in), chalk the edges and punch holes to correspond with those of the cover.

4 Print the titles for your photos on patterned paper and cut to form mini flags. Chalk the edges and glue to the relevant pages.

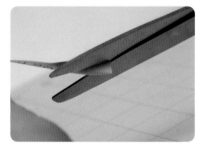

5 Adhere your photos and decorate the pages with chipboard pieces and other embellishments before binding everything together with the binder rings.

Memories in a jar

YOU WILL NEED

Trimmer
Ultra ShapeXpress™ and circle template
Glass jar
Ruler
Discarded novel with discoloured pages
Ribbon
1 vintage flower
Brown chalk
Scrapbook adhesive

The vintage look, aged, brownish and rustic, was ideal for this glass jar filled with memories of my grandmother. This is the ideal project for using those black and white photos of many years ago. Add your own special memorabilia to the bottle once you've inserted the printed pages. If you cannot bring yourself to tear pages (even from a discarded book), use patterned paper with a print finish instead.

1 Clean the glass jar and dry thoroughly. Measure the height of the jar.

2 Tear three pages from the book. Trim these to the desired size (if necessary) and chalk the edges.

3 Place the paper inside the bottle and add your vintage photos and any other memorabilia, if you wish.

4 Close the lid and tie the ribbons around the neck of the jar, finishing with a lavish bow.

5 Use the Ultra ShapeXpress™ and circle shape template to cut a circle to fit the lid, chalk the edges and adhere to the top of the lid using scrapbook adhesive.

6 Finish with the vintage flower.

Canvas mini book

YOU WILL NEED

Trimmer

Craft mat

Craft drill

2 blocked white canvas squares of 10 cm (3.9 in)

A sheet of foam core

Craft paint (blue and white)

Paintbrush

Embellishments

Organza ribbon for binding

Metal plate and tabs with title (I used 7gypsies)

Printable patterned paper (I used houseof3)

Chalk

Scrapbook adhesive

I Apply blue paint to both sides of the canvases, allow to dry and dry-brush the sides with white paint.

2 Cut the foam core into 10 cm (3.9 in) squares and chalk all the edges.

3 Drill holes through the covers and foam core inners 2 cm (0.8 in) from the top and bottom.

4 Print your printable kit papers and trim to fit the canvas and foam core squares. Chalk all the sides and adhere to the foam and canvas. Add your titles and further embellishments to the pages.

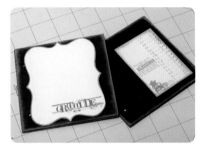

5 Assemble and bind the book by threading the ribbon through the holes from the bottom up and tying a beautiful bow on the front.

Canvas has been used for several projects in this book, all of them quite diverse. "So why not make a canvas album?" I thought. I used two small blocked canvas squares for the front and back cover, and foam core for the inside pages. My very useful Fiskars drill made holes for the organza ribbon, which was used to bind everything together in no time.

Framed brotherly love

1 Remove the glass and backing from the back of the frames and measure the size of the window where you will add your photo.

2 Trim the photo to size and place in one frame behind the glass. Replace the backing and close the frame completely.

3 Adhere the chipboard letters to the glass of the photo frame, so your title will be on the outside of the glass and the photo on the inside.

4 Trim the patterned paper to the size of the photo area. Embellish with accents and words of your choice. I chose the word *love*. Place the embellished sheet in the frame and complete in the same way as the photo.

This photo of my youngest brother and me has always been very dear to me. To turn it into something more than just a framed photo, I scrapped it in its frame, with a companion frame symbolising love and affection. These gorgeous frames are widely available.

Pretty practical tins

YOU WILL NEED

Trimmer

Craft mat

3 empty, cleaned food tins

Ruler

3 sheets of patterned paper
(I used echo park paper co)

Alpha and border sticker sheet
(from echo park paper co)

Chalk

Scrapbook adhesive

Recycled pea, sweet corn and jam tins have a myriad uses. Unadorned they are dead ugly, but who says they have to stay that way? Soak in water to remove their labels, clean them thoroughly and ensure that there are no sharp edges left where the tops were removed before you start. There are so many bright and cheerful papers to choose from, that I had great fun making my selection to turn the tins into pretty practical containers for everyday items.

I Measure the height and circumference of your tins and cut three varieties of patterned paper rectangles to fit comfortably around each tin. Chalk the edges.

2 Stick down a matching scalloped border, from the border sticker sheet, around the top edge of each patterned paper cover.

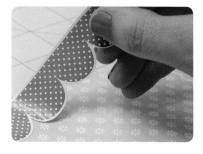

3 Using the alpha stickers stick down titles on the patterned paper, for example *pens* or *scissors* or whatever the contents of the tins are likely to be. Cut flags from red paper scraps and adhere to either side of the titles.

4 Adhere the prepared paper covers to the tins, taking care that they fit snugly around the tins.

Significant keys

1 Remove the backing and glass of the frame. Measure the inside, cut a piece of patterned paper to fit and adhere before reassembling the frame without the glass.

2 Screw in the metal hook in the centre just below the top of the frame.

3 Hang the red metal heart and one word key on the hook.

4 Adhere the chipboard charm with the wording *our home* below the red metal heart. Chalk edges of the frame accent and adhere to frame the wording.

5 Finish off with a circle chipboard charm and adhere a second word key using Dodz.

The most important keys in any woman's life must be the key to her heart and the key to her home. I played with this idea when I made this vintage frame. I used word keys from the Tim Holtz idea-ology range, but you could just as easily use real keys and have the decorative frame double as a real key holder.

Recipe tin

Using a tin for special recipes is fun and practical – just add to your collection, and when one tin is filled to the brim, decorate a second one. A decorated recipe tin also makes a super gift for family and friends. And if you need a gift for someone who does not like cooking and baking, change your wording and fill the tin with freshly baked muffins, cookies or home made fudge. You can be sure the tin will skip the cupboard and receive a beautiful front row position!

1 Measure the top of the tin. Cut patterned paper to size, round the corners, chalk and adhere to the tin. Repeat for the inside of the lid.

2 Measure the sides, cut patterned paper to size, chalk and adhere. If you need to use more than one sheet of paper, ensure that your pattern aligns perfectly, overlapping it slightly.

3 Decorate the top of the tin with more patterned paper and ribbon. Cut a piece of felt to size for the top of the tin and scallop the edge.

4 Print the title on cardstock, cut out and adhere to the scalloped felt, adding some ribbon and a brad. Glue to the top of the tin.

5 Print headings for recipe sub-sections on cardstock and cut out. Cut dividers from cardstock just smaller than the width of the tin and adhere the sub-section headings to the dividers. Cut strips of felt to be used as tabs, and staple into position on the dividers.

6 Print your recipes, cut to size and assemble, with the dividers, to place in the tin.

7 Finish off with a ribbon around the tin, tied in a beautiful bow.

Blackboard wedding collection

YOU WILL NEED

2 wooden frames

Blackboard paint

Photos

Ribbon and other memorabilia

Scrapbook adhesive

1 Remove the backing and glass from the frames. Apply several layers of blackboard paint to the backing and allow to dry.

2 Reassemble the frames without the glass. Arrange your photos on the backing, leaving space for comments if you wish, and adhere.

4 Once your frames are hanging on the wall, decide if you want to add some fabric from your dress or a special bunting draped over the top to add a lovely finishing touch to a special collection.

Wooden frames filled with photos tell the story of our lives. These particular frames hold treasured memories of our wedding day. I painted the backing with blackboard paint not only for effect, but also to be able to write comments under the various photos using chalk. The two large frames have space for several photos and are virtually an album on the wall. I added my tiara to the collection. If you have dried and preserved flowers from your boquet, they will also make a striking addition.

3 Add suitable embellishments and memorabilia to the photos and frame. I attached my tiara to the frame using ribbon. You may want to add other elements.

Baking sheet recipe holder

YOU WILL NEED

Trimmer

Craft mat

Metal baking tin

Sandpaper

Spray paint

Ruler

Large corner rounder

2 sheets of cardstock

1 sheet of patterned paper
(I used Heidi Swapp)

Ribbon

Chipboard alpha letters

Clear accent
(I used Heidi Swapp)

Doily

Brads

Chalk

Scrapbook adhesive

I absolutely love baking; it's a habit and way of life that keeps me entertained in the kitchen for hours on end. My other passion is scrapbooking, so using scrapbooking techniques to turn an old baking tin into a recipe holder came naturally. This beauty hangs in my kitchen, but is sure to be a much appreciated gift.

1 Sand the baking tin, wipe clean and spray paint. Leave to dry. Lightly sand again to create a distressed look.

2 Decorate the inside of the tin with clear accents at the top. Add a ribbon running all the way down, and adhere the lettering.

3 Measure the inside of the tin and trim patterned paper slightly smaller than this size, round the corners, then chalk and adhere to the tin to fit below the title.

4 Print your recipes on cardstock and cut slightly smaller than the backing paper. Add a photo and embellishments for each recipe.

5 Assemble the recipes using a doily and brads and finally adhere to the backing sheet with adhesive.

baking

Red Velvet Cake

Ingredients:
- 1/2 cup butter
- 1 1/2 cups sugar
- 2 eggs
- 2 tbsp cocoa
- 2 tbsp red food colouring
- 1 tsp salt
- 2 1/2 cups flour
- 1 tsp vanilla extract
- 1 cup buttermilk
- 1 tsp baking soda
- 1 tbsp vinegar

Method:

Cream the butter then beat in the sugar gradually.
Add the eggs - one at a time - beating well after each addition.
Make a paste of the cocoa and food colouring and add to the
creamed mixture.
Add the salt, flour, vanilla extract and buttermilk, beating well
after each addition.
Sprinkle the baking soda over the vinegar and then pour the
vinegar over the batter.
Mix well.
Divide the mixture into 2 cake tins and bake for 30 minutes at 180ºC.

Icing:

Cream 200g plain cream cheese and 1/4 cup softened butter, and then
gradually add in 1 cup caster sugar and 1/4 cup of cocoa and finally 1 tsp vanilla
extract.

Mesh wire note-frames

1 Remove the backing and glass from the frames. Cut the mesh to fit the frame and adhere in the corners using the screws.

2 Measure the inside of the frame and cut the patterned paper to size. Place over the wire and replace the backing of the frame.

3 Add your title to one frame using the clips and fill the other frame with keepsakes in the same way.

4 Finally hang these pretty note-holders somewhere visually appealing or wrap them and give them to someone special who will be sure to treasure them.

Framed mesh makes a small but most effective and unusual note holder and looks pretty to boot. Both mesh wire and frames are readily available from your local DIY store and the project itself can be completed in a jiffy.

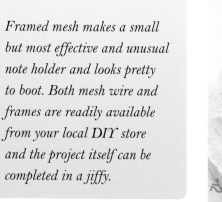

Jaclyn Venter worked in PR and marketing for many years before becoming a Fiskars-certified brand ambassador. Better known as Fisk-a-teer #1287, she teaches all the Fiskars scrapbooking classes in South Africa as part of their global programme to promote crafting. She has featured in various local and international online media, the *Show me how craft* programme on the Home channel of DSTV and writes several blogs. She specifically develops projects around new tools and has won many prizes for her creative work. Most of her time is spent with photographs, paper and glue in her craft studio, or in the kitchen where she enjoys her other passion – baking. Her mean carrot cake is to die for. She also owns and runs two small businesses. Jaclyn is married and lives in Centurion.